GRANDMOTHERS
ARE LIKE
SNOWFLAKES

. . . NO TWO ARE ALIKE

GRANDMOTHERS ARE LIKE SNOWFLAKES

...NO TWO ARE ALIKE

JANET LANESE

A Dell Trade Paperback

A DELL TRADE PAPERBACK
Published by
Dell Publishing
a division of
Bantam Doubleday Dell Publishing Group, Inc.
1540 Broadway
New York, New York 10036

Copyright © 1996 by Janet Lanese

The trademark Dell® is registered in the U.S. Patent and Trademark Office.

Library of Congress Cataloging in Publication Data
Grandmothers are like snowflakes—no two are alike / [compiled by] Janet Lanese.
p.   cm.
ISBN 0-440-50717-0
1. Grandmothers—Quotations, maxims, etc.   I. Lanese, Janet.
PN6084.G6G74   1996
306.874´5—dc20   95-38616
CIP
Printed in the United States of America
Published simultaneously in Canada
May 1996
10   9   8   7   6   5
FFG

DEDICATION

To all the wonderful grandmothers who
have made a difference in their
grandchildren's lives.

And to the greatest grandmother of them
all, my mother,
Maryon (Melé) Mackie.

ACKNOWLEDGMENTS

Thanks to Vera Allen-Smith and Joyce K. Allen
Logan, my two computer wizards and editors
who were indispensable.
Thanks also to my literary agent,
Laurie Harper of Sebastian Agency, who is my
greatest ally, and to Mary Ellen O'Neill and Trish
Todd, my talented editors from Dell Publishing,
who were joys to work with.

CONTENTS

GRANDMAS THEN AND NOW

It is as grandmothers that our mothers come into the fullness of their grace. When a man's mother holds his child in her gladden arms he is aware of the roundness of life's cycle; of the mystic harmony of life's ways.

Christopher Morley

The birth of a child in the family can be the greatest leveler of differences, bringing everyone together.

Grandma Jan

Grandma's home is her grandchildren's second home, a sort of security blanket they can escape to when the world is unfriendly.

Grandma Jan

Parent-child relationships are complex. Grandmother-grandchild relationships are simple. Grandmas are short on criticism and long on love.

Grandma Jan

What's so simple even a small child can
manipulate it?
  Why, a grandmother, of course!

Anonymous

If you would civilize a man, begin with his
grandmother.

Victor Hugo

5

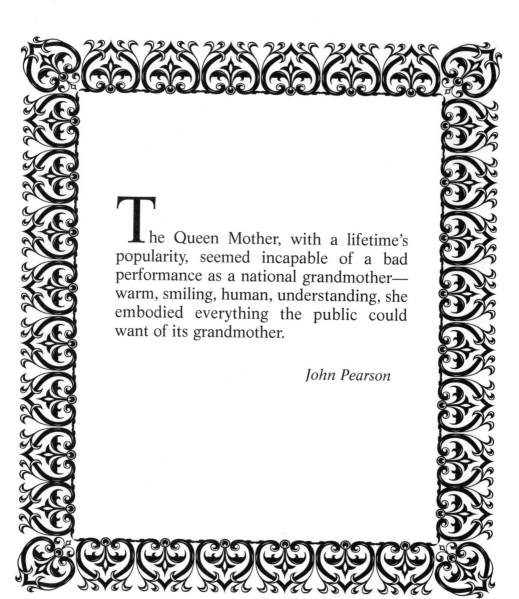

The Queen Mother, with a lifetime's popularity, seemed incapable of a bad performance as a national grandmother—warm, smiling, human, understanding, she embodied everything the public could want of its grandmother.

John Pearson

Since the beginning of time grandmothers
have been negotiators and peacemakers in
their families.

Grandma Jan

The closest friends I have made all through
life have been people who also grew up
close to a loved and loving grandmother or
grandfather.

Margaret Mead

C̲hildren have more need of models
than critics.

Joseph Joubert

Children have never been very
good at listening to their elders,
but they have never failed to
imitate them.

James Baldwin

All children wear the sign:

I want to be important NOW!

Many of our juvenile delinquency problems arise because nobody reads the sign.

Dan Pursuit

If a child lives with approval, he learns to live with himself.

 Dorothy Law Nolte

In order not to influence a child, one must be careful not to be that child's parent or grandparent.

Don Marquis

━━━━━━━━━━

If children grew up according to early indications, we should have nothing but geniuses.

Goethe

Children's children are a crown to the aged,
and parents are the pride of their children.

Proverbs 17:6

Grandchildren restore our zest for life, and
our faith in humanity.

Grandma Jan

ld-fashioned grandmothers take their grandchildren by the hand and lead them into the future. They are safe and kind, and wiser than the child's mother.

Florence King

Our grandchildren accept us for ourselves, without rebuke or effort to change us, as no one in our entire lives has ever done, not our parents, siblings, spouses, friends—and hardly ever our own grown children.

Ruth Goode

The person who has lived the most is not the one with the most years, but the one with the richest experiences.

Jean-Jacques Rousseau

God gave us loving grandchildren as a reward for all our random acts of kindness.

Grandma Jan

There are one hundred and fifty-two
distinctly different ways of holding a baby,
and they are all right.

Heywood Broun

Whether she is a homemaker
or career woman, all a
grandmother wants is
her family's love and
respect as a
productive individual
who has much to
contribute.

Grandma Jan

Grandchildren don't make a woman feel old; it's being married to a grandfather that bothers her.

Grandma Jan

That flamboyant grandmother wearing black leather and riding a Harley may not fit the picture of an old-fashioned granny, yet she is a confident and free-spirited woman. Her children call her eccentric, but her grandkids call her "cool!"

Grandma Jan

A grandmother is a baby-sitter who watches the kids instead of the television.

Anonymous

Grandchildren are loving reminders of what we're really here for.

Grandma Jan

Grandmothers are voices of the past and role models of the present. Grandmothers open the doors to the future.

Helen Ketchum

My grandmothers are full of memories.

Margaret Walker

My grandma's life was so exciting, it would make a great TV miniseries.

Nathan (age ten)

My great-grandmama told my grandmama the part she lived through that my grandmama didn't live through and my grandmama told my mama what they both lived through and my mama told me what they all lived through and we're supposed to pass it down like that from generation to generation so we'll never forget.

Gayl Jones

It is the malady of our age that the young are so busy teaching us that they have no time left to learn.

Eric Hoffer

———

I love my grandma's wrinkles. Every one tells a story.

Tammy (age eight)

Let's bring back grandmothers! A real
family consists of three generations. It's
time Americans stopped worrying about
interference and being a burden on the
children and regrouped under one roof.

Florence King

It's impossible for a grandmother to
understand that few people, and maybe
none, will find her grandchild as endearing
as she does.

Grandma Jan

19

What families have in common the world around is that they are the place where people learn who they are and how to be that way.

Jean-Illsley Clark

Being a grandmother is our last chance to act like a kid without being accused of being in our second childhood.

Grandma Jan

At Nana's house even my puppy who piddles is welcomed with love.

Dennis (age seven)

When Grandma was a girl, she didn't do things the girls do today. But then the grandmas didn't do the things grandmas do today.

Anonymous

Perfection is in the eyes of those who wear blinders, and nobody wears blinders better than a doting grandmother.

Grandma Jan

The Perks of Grandmotherhood

❤ Your maternal instincts are rekindled

❤ You appreciate the continuity of life

❤ You experience the joy of unconditional love

❤ You start mellowing out

❤ You live every day to its fullest

❤ You're closer to your family

❤ You accept the things you cannot change

❤ You pay attention to your own physical and emotional well-being

❤ You make time for travel and romance

Grandma Jan

Wow! Are grandchildren great! Spoil them rotten—give them back—and laugh and laugh. Revenge is sweet!

Aris Painter

Was there ever a grandparent bushed after a day of minding noisy youngsters who hasn't felt the Lord knew what He was doing when He gave little children to young people?

Joe E. Wells

MUTUAL ATTRACTION

I could never understand why people were so batty over their grandchildren until mine came into my life. Everything they do, everything they are is precious. I'm looking forward to watching them grow, watching them become.

Sally Stuart

Feeding our grandbabies, burping them, bathing them, changing them, singing to them and cuddling them, are all expressions of our love.

That love is returned to us tenfold before they take their first step.

Grandma Jan

The joys of the grandparent-grandchild
bond, the double joys of trust and love.

Grandma Jan

I'm sure my grandmother is reincarnated—
she knows too much.

Michael (age thirteen)

Who can resist seeing oneself in miniature?
It is inevitable that your adorable grandbaby
inherits dimples, curly hair, and a button
nose from your side of the family.

Grandma Jan

The only ones who don't notice when your
hair starts graying, your face is sagging, and
your waistline is disappearing are your
grandchildren and the family dog.

Grandma Jan

You know you have been bitten by the grandmother bug when you

♥ See the beauty in a red, wizened newborn's face

♥ Wallpaper the den in Disney characters

♥ Send those ugly hospital baby photos to all your friends and relatives

♥ Pick up your "Grandma's Brag Book" and it's heavier than the family album

♥ Buy the baby a wardrobe whose cost rivals the national debt

♥ Offer to baby-sit on your Bingo night

♥ Start collecting teddy bears

♥ Trade in your sports car for a minivan with a built-in baby seat

♥ Find yourself using baby talk to your husband, until he threatens to "wing your wittle neck"

Grandma Jan

I really don't think of my grandmother as old, only well seasoned.

Maggie (age fourteen)

A person's maturity consists in having found again the seriousness one had as a child at play.

Friedrich Wilhelm Nietzsche

Grandmothers are natural baby-sitters. Who is more trustworthy or whose fee is more nominal? For us it is a labor of love.

Grandma Jan

For an old lady, my grandmother's memory is unbelievable. She has eighteen grandchildren and she still remembers all of our names.

Brian (age twelve)

You had no choice about what your given name would be, and you'll probably have about the same chance of influencing your grandchildren about what they will call you. As long as they call you. Grandma, Nana, Mi Mi, and Ounma are all terms of endearment.

Grandma Jan

I love the way my Mi Mi smells. It's sort of a mixture of fresh-baked brownies and that rose perfume old people wear.

Jessica (age ten)

Grandmothers and their grandchildren always seem to be on the same wavelength. Only grandmothers appreciate how wise children are and how much children understand about the world around them.

Grandma Jan

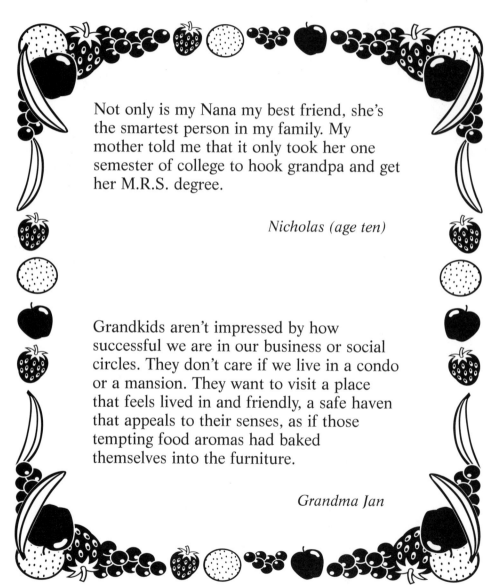

Not only is my Nana my best friend, she's the smartest person in my family. My mother told me that it only took her one semester of college to hook grandpa and get her M.R.S. degree.

Nicholas (age ten)

Grandkids aren't impressed by how successful we are in our business or social circles. They don't care if we live in a condo or a mansion. They want to visit a place that feels lived in and friendly, a safe haven that appeals to their senses, as if those tempting food aromas had baked themselves into the furniture.

Grandma Jan

What Is a Grandmother?
by Patsy Gray (age nine)

A grandmother is a lady who has no children of her own so she likes other people's little girls. A grandfather is a man grandmother. He goes for walks with the boys, and they talk about fishing and tractors, and things like that. Grandmothers don't have to do anything except be there. They're old, so they shouldn't play hard or run. It is enough if they drive us to the market where the pretend horse is and have lots of dimes ready. Or, if they take us for walks, they should slow down past things like pretty leaves and caterpillars. They should never say "Hurry up!"

Usually they are fat, but not too fat to tie a kid's shoes. They wear glasses and funny underwear. They can take their teeth and gums off.

It's better if they don't typewrite or play cards except with us. They don't have to be smart, only answer questions like why dogs hate cats, and how come God isn't married.

They don't talk baby talk like visitors do

because it is hard to understand. When they read to us, they don't skip or mind if it is the same story again.

Everybody should try to have one, especially if you don't have television, because grandmothers are the only grown-ups who have time.

Ruth Goode

My Nana can run the microwave better than any person I know.

Mark (age six)

If grandmas hadn't existed, kids would have inevitably invented them.

Arthur Kornhaber, M.D.

Though the world has changed around us, grandmothers and grandchildren still share an emotional bond that is one of life's most powerful experiences.

Grandma Jan

My grandma is so great, she's almost worth her weight in chocolate fudge brownies.

Jeffrey (age eleven)

Children love to laugh, to be around grown-ups who can laugh at themselves and at life. Grandmothers have learned the more laughter they have in their lives, the better. That's why grandmothers keep children's spirits soaring.

Grandma Jan

 My grandma and Santa Claus are my very favorite people. I think they're about the same age.

Jessica (age five)

Some of my best friends are children. In fact, all of my best friends are children.

J. D. Salinger

My grandma is the funnest person I know. She goes to all my ball games, plays Monopoly with me, and takes me to Disneyland.

Marcy (age six)

Grandmothers rarely get disheartened about their grandchildren's mistakes. Grandmothers regard their grandchildren's blunders merely as stepping-stones to success.

Grandma Jan

All elders should have at least one youngster to be "crazy about" and vice versa. Grandparenting supplies the role model for a healthy and fulfilling old age. And grandchildren want grandparents.

Arthur Kornhaber, M.D.

I love my grandma because no matter how many stupid things I do, she still tells all her friends that I am the smartest boy alive.

Mark (age seven)

Your sons weren't made to like you. That's
what grandchildren are for.

Jane Smiley

Every child comes with the message that
God is not yet discouraged of man.

Rabindranath Tagore

Why are grandmothers nicer than mothers?
Because they don't believe in spanking,
that's why!

Melanie (age six)

THAT MAGIC
TOUCH

When it seems the world can't understand,
Your grandmother's there to hold your
hand.

With her gentle words and open heart
Your grandmother shares with graceful art.

Her adoring eyes see just the best
Your grandmother will ignore the rest.

A grandmother's love means oh, so much!
Your grandmother has that magic touch.

Joyce K. Allen Logan

It is our right as grandmothers to love unconditionally.

Grandma Jan

Grandchildren have the magic of putting the fun back into middle age.

Grandma Jan

How wonderful to have Grandma to complain to when I'm mad at my parents.

Carolyn (age ten)

Every grandmother enriches her grandchildren's lives in her own special way.

Grandma Jan

Like the sun, a grandmother's love shines on her grandchildren, nourishing their emotional and spiritual growth.

Grandma Jan

No other family member can encourage, support, and boost a child's self-esteem like a grandmother.

Grandma Jan

A truly appreciative child will break, lose, spoil or fondle to death any really successful gift within a matter of minutes.

Russell Lynes

Nothing offends children more than to play down to them. All the greatest children's books—*The Pilgrim's Progress, Robinson Crusoe, Grimm's Fairy Tales* and *Gulliver's Travels*—were written for adults.

George Bernard Shaw

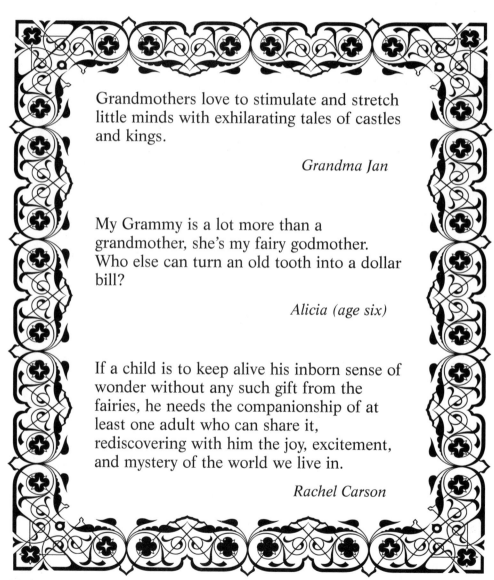

Grandmothers love to stimulate and stretch little minds with exhilarating tales of castles and kings.

Grandma Jan

My Grammy is a lot more than a grandmother, she's my fairy godmother. Who else can turn an old tooth into a dollar bill?

Alicia (age six)

If a child is to keep alive his inborn sense of wonder without any such gift from the fairies, he needs the companionship of at least one adult who can share it, rediscovering with him the joy, excitement, and mystery of the world we live in.

Rachel Carson

No one has yet fully realized the wealth of sympathy, kindness, and generosity hidden in the soul of a child. The effort of every true education should be to unlock that treasure.

Emma Goldman

===============

Nothing brings greater joy to grandchildren and grandmothers than entering together into a world of fantasy and wonder.

Grandma Jan

===============

There is still a child in all of us who has always believed in miracles. To children miracles are simple things. Every day is miraculous—unexplained, inspiring, ever new.

Karen Goldman

Children know the grace of God better than most of us. They see the world the way the morning brings it back to them. New and born and fresh and wonderful.

Archibald MacLeish

A grandmother's love is a powerful potion.

Grandma Jan

A Grandma's Lullaby

Little one, precious one,
　　Time to go off to sleep now.

Hush-a-bye, don't you cry,
　　Time to go off to Dreamland.

Morning will come and your sunshine smile
　　Lights our hearts so sweetly.

Little one, precious one,
　　Grandma loves you forever.

Ann M. Sherman-Simpson

What children expect from grandparents is
not to be understood but to be loved.

Grandma Jan

So many things we love are you!

I can't seem to explain except
by little things, but flowers and
beautiful handmade things—Small stitches

So much of reading and thinking—
so many sweet customs and so much of
our . . . well, our religion. It is all you.

I hadn't realized it before. This is so
vague but do you see a little, dear
Grandma? I want to thank you.

from "Bring Me a Unicorn"
by Anne Morrow Lindbergh

> A grandmother magically uses her grandchildren's eyes and hearts to see and feel as they do. She tries to see things from their point of view.
>
> *Grandma Jan*

Grandmothers love questions like

❤ Which cows give chocolate milk?

❤ Is there really a man in the moon?

❤ How do birds fly?

❤ Does the Easter bunny lay eggs?

❤ If the earth is round, why don't we fall off?

❤ Do flowers sleep at night?

Grandma Jan

A grandmother's patience is a like a tube of toothpaste—never quite all gone.

Grandma Jan

A grandmother is an overly fussy person who spits on her handkerchief and wipes imaginary smudges off your face.

Kimberly (age eight)

Family faces are magic mirrors. Looking at people who belong to us, we see the past, present, and future.

Gail Lumet Buckley

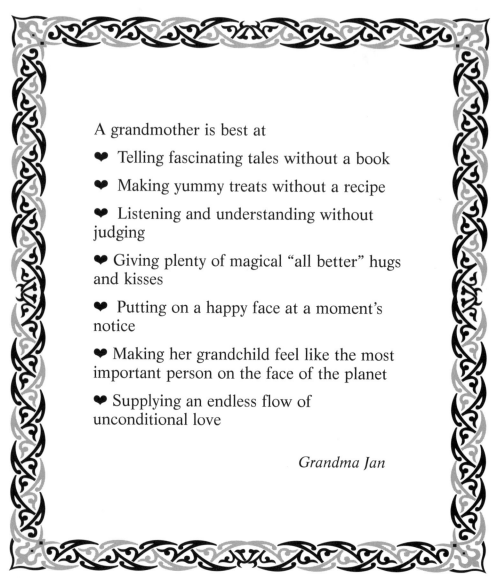

A grandmother is best at

❤ Telling fascinating tales without a book

❤ Making yummy treats without a recipe

❤ Listening and understanding without judging

❤ Giving plenty of magical "all better" hugs and kisses

❤ Putting on a happy face at a moment's notice

❤ Making her grandchild feel like the most important person on the face of the planet

❤ Supplying an endless flow of unconditional love

Grandma Jan

If nothing is going well, call your grandmother or grandfather.

Italian proverb

Hugs and kisses are even grander when they are given by a loving grandmother.

Grandma Jan

Once you've loved a child, you will love all children. You give away your love to one, and you find that by giving you've made yourself an inexhaustible treasury.

Margaret Lee Runbeck

The secret that makes grandma's cooking taste so terrific is that she always adds a spoonful of love.

Grandma Jan

Grandmothers are like Kleenex: soft, strong and able to absorb the hurts of a small child.

Grandma Jan

Grandma was kind of a first-aid station, or a Red Cross nurse, who took up where the battle ended, accepting us and our little sobbing sins, gathering the whole of us into her lap, restoring us to health and confidence by her amazing faith in life, and in a mortal's strength to use it.

Lillian Smith

My Nana is the only person in the whole world that I let hold my tongue down with a stick, give me nasty-tasting medicine, and put a thermometer in a place I shouldn't mention.

Jason (age six)

Grandmothers of every race and country have a legendary role as healers: Jewish grandmothers make chicken soup, others have their own special remedies. When a child in a North American Yurok Indian tribe is ill, Grandmother goes out into the wilderness to intervene with the spirits by singing and speaking to them. Every grandmother has her own song.

Arthur Kornhaber, M.D.

Out of love, parents teach their children to be wary of new things. Out of love, grandmothers encourage their grandchildren to take a chance and conquer the unknown.

Grandma Jan

Grandma begs my parents to go out for the evening so she can be alone with me.

Sarah (age four)

A grandchild represents a world in us, a world nonexistent before his birth. Once a grandmother, a woman is reborn into a new world, one filled with hope and expectations.

Grandma Jan

Grandmothering comes not from the head but from the heart.

Grandma Jan

OUR LITTLE ANGELS

A baby is God's opinion that the world should go on.

Carl Sandburg

A newborn baby . . . is without question the most phenomenal, the most astonishing, the most absolutely unparalleled thing that has yet occurred in the entire history of this planet.

Irvin S. Cobb

Babies are such a nice way to start people.

Don Herold

Something to live for came to place
  Something to die for maybe

Something to give even sorrow a grace
  And yet it was only a baby

Harriet Spofford

─────────────

Every baby born into the world is a finer
one than the last.

Charles Dickens

─────────────

The secret of a happy life is to skip having
children and go directly to the
grandchildren.

Momma
(cartoon character created by Mel Lazarus)

It is the rare grandmother who doesn't think her grandchild is constantly growing toward the pinnacle of perfection.

Grandma Jan

The first grandchild is a thrill, but the second and third ones are just as delightful. Each one is a fresh, unique personality, a tiny but distinct human being whom you've never known before.

Grandma Jan

Rapture and euphoria are weak attempts at describing the bliss I felt watching the birth of my granddaughter.

Vera Allen-Smith

Children are like puppies; you have to keep
them near you and look after them if you
want their affection.

Anna Magnani

Children divine those who love them; it is a
gift of nature which we lose as we grow up.

Paul de Kock

Even if the first third of your life was
dominated by your parents, and the second
third by your children, you still have your
grandchildren to salvage the remainder.

Grandma Jan

Not all of us think grandkids are the greatest—but that was before I met mine.

Jane Russell

My three grandchildren, Christopher, Melanie, and Matthew, are the perfect age—too old for strollers and too young to borrow my car.

Grandma Jan

The kind sweet souls who love, cherish, inspire and protect their grandchildren are not guardian angels; they are grandmothers.

Bettye "Mi Mi" Flynn

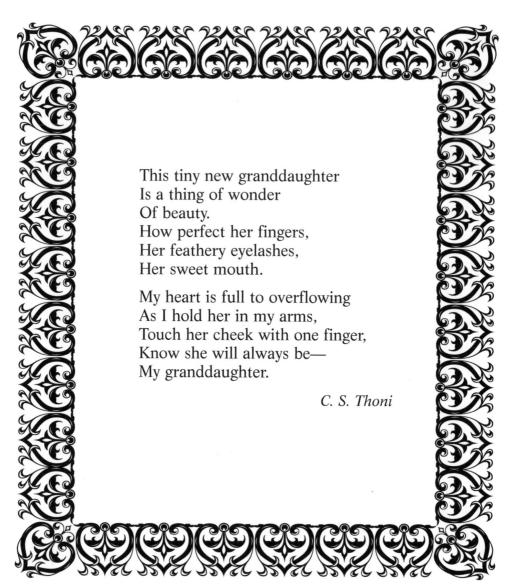

This tiny new granddaughter
Is a thing of wonder
Of beauty.
How perfect her fingers,
Her feathery eyelashes,
Her sweet mouth.

My heart is full to overflowing
As I hold her in my arms,
Touch her cheek with one finger,
Know she will always be—
My granddaughter.

C. S. Thoni

A new grandson
Our family line moves on
How beautiful this day
How wonderful this child
With such shining eyes
And smooth skin.

A new grandson
Brings joy and hope
For a brighter, happier future.

C. S. Thoni

Children are likely to live up to what
you believe of them.

Lady Bird Johnson

Dearer than our children are the children of our children.

Egyptian proverb

 Grandchildren are magical creatures you can lock out of your kitchen, but never out of your heart.

Grandma Jan

This grandchild, so new and small,
    with tiny hands and large bright eyes
Brings life to the world, a fresh beginning
    filled with endless surprises and new
    discoveries.

The fullness of life shines in this tiny face,
    familiar features: nose and chin, a
    dimpled cheek
Bring love and joy to life. A family grows
    toward a future of possibility and
    promise.

Joyce K. Allen Logan

Perfect love sometimes does not come until the first grandchild.

Welsh proverb

I'm not a picture-toting grandma—but my grandchildren just happen to be the best-looking children in the continental United States, and you can throw in Canada and the Virgin Islands.

Abigail Van Buren

A grandmother proudly wheeled her grandchild into the park. An acquaintance came by, peeked into the carriage and said, "My, what a gorgeous child!"

The grandmother said, "Wait until you see her pictures!"

Milton Berle

My grandkids' visits are special times, filled
with lots of hugs and kisses, sighs and cries.
I enjoy these times, but it's still a relief to
know their parents will take over again at
the end of the day.

Barbara Wallis

By the time the youngest children have
learned to keep the place tidy, the oldest
grandchildren are on hand to tear it to
pieces.

Christopher Morley

What feeling is so nice as a child's hand in
yours? So small, so soft and warm, like a
kitten huddling in the shelter of your clasp.

Marjorie Holmes

How to Eat Like a Child

Spinach:

1. Divide into little piles. Rearrange again into new piles.

2. After five or six maneuvers, sit back and say you are full.

Ice-cream cone:

1. Ask for a double scoop. Knock the top scoop off while walking out the door of the ice-cream parlor. Cry.

2. Lick the remaining scoop slowly so that the ice cream melts down the outside of the cone and over your hand. Stop licking when the ice cream is even with the top of the cone. Be sure it is absolutely even.

3. Eat a hole in the bottom of the cone and suck the rest of the ice cream out of the bottom.

4. When only the cone remains with ice cream coating the inside, leave on car dashboard.

Chocolate-chip cookies:
1. Half-sit, half-lie on the bed, propped up by a pillow. Read a book. Place cookies next to you on the sheet so that the crumbs get in the bed.

2. As you eat the cookies, remove each chocolate chip and place it on your stomach.

3. When all the cookies are consumed, eat the chips one by one, allowing two per page.

Delia Ephron

My Granddaughter Is . . .

A bell of laughter shattering
  the morning sun

A crystal gift of tears for me
  to wipe away

A present joy that now is more
  than I can ever say

A promise of a future when
  my days are done

Dorcas Moyer

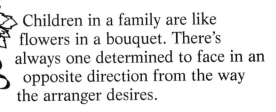 Children in a family are like
flowers in a bouquet. There's
always one determined to face in an
opposite direction from the way
the arranger desires.

Madeline Cox

A grandma is a bossy lady who orders you to put on a sweater when she's chilly and to go to bed when she's tired—tired of you, that is.

Mark (age nine)

The persons hardest to convince they're at retirement age are children at bedtime.

Shanon Fife

Children ask better questions than do adults. "May I have a cookie?" "Why is the sky blue?" and "What does a cow say?" are far more likely to elicit a cheerful response than "Where's your manuscript?" and "Who's your lawyer?"

Fran Lebowitz

As long as her grandchild is having fun playing games, a grandmother doesn't place a lot of emphasis on winning. But don't let another adult criticize the little tyke! It's no wonder grandmas and Little League umpires don't get along.

Grandma Jan

Heirlooms we don't have in our family. But stories we've got.

Kim Chernin

My grandma tells me she keeps the family skeletons in the closet, but I've looked and looked and I still can't find them.

Sarah (age five)

You know children are growing up when they start asking questions that have answers.

John J. Plomp

Just how ambitious was Grandma Jones when it came to her grandchildren? Well, when a stranger inquired as to their ages, she replied, "The doctor's in the third grade and the rocket scientist is in the fifth."

Anonymous

My grandma looks exactly like my mom, only more lumpy.

Jonathan (age eight)

Grandchildren are a renewal of life, a little bit of us going on into the future.

Helene Schellenberg Barnhart

Grandmothers are older than they look. I heard many of them go back to World War II.

Susan (age nine)

What Is a Grandson?

A grandson is that other man in Grandmother's life who has her wrapped right around his finger. A bewitching creature sprinkled with stardust, a grandson is heaven-sent, and only one step below perfection. A grandson is purity in dirty sneakers, chivalry on a carousel horse, and beauty with a milk mustache. No matter how small his size, a grandson is big in spirit.

A grandson is a player of nonsensical computer games, a dreamer of flights to other galaxies, and an avid collector of useless trinkets. A quick study in perpetual motion, a grandson pauses long enough to gulp down a snack, glance at the TV, flip through a comic book, or eavesdrop on Grandmother's telephone conversation.

A grandson is a gentle prankster with an impish grin and a jolly laugh whose spontaneous wit keeps Grandmother on her toes. Though he dismisses Grandmother's bear hugs and wet kisses as "baby stuff," a grandson never fails to tell her that she is the best grandma in the world. A grandson is the captor who holds the key to Grandmother's heart.

Grandma Jan

What Is a Granddaughter?

A granddaughter is the most exciting thing that can happen to an empty-nester. A charismatic angel with slightly frayed wings, she fills Grandmother's home with energetic activity and contagious laughter. Where there is love, there is usually a granddaughter near by.

A granddaughter is grace on Rollerblades, independence parading around in father's best shirt, and brilliance building sand castles. A granddaughter is Grandmother's closest confidante and best friend. Enchanting, amusing, inquisitive, and wise beyond her years, a granddaughter has the power to renew Grandmother's spirit and expand her universe in a twinkle of an eye.

A granddaughter is a pint-sized bolt of lightning who relishes turning Grandmother's daily routine topsy-turvy. If a granddaughter is not bombarding Grandmother with hypothetical questions or begging her to play ball, she's into the cookie jar. But when she finally winds down, climbs up on Grandmother's lap, and whispers those magical words "Hold me, Grandma," a granddaughter is pure bliss.

Grandma Jan

Reflection

Tonight my small grandson
Consults the mirror.
With five-year-old aplomb
He condenses the universe
Into that shining square.

One light winks out.
A shadow falls across his face.
His fingers touch one cheek, still bright.
"This is morning," he says,
"And this is night."

The enormity of earth is tailored
To fit in his reflection.
His glance compresses ages, solves mysteries.
I find in his features, briefly seen there
The same answer he finds in the mirror.

Dorcas Moyer

A grandchild should never be loved for love returned; a grandchild should be loved for himself, and nothing else.

Grandma Jan

A grandmother is a woman who's thrilled because her grandchild can recite the Gettysburg Address at eight when Lincoln didn't do it until he was much older.

Milton Berle

Children are remarkable for their intelligence and ardor, for their curiosity, their intolerance of shams, the clarity and ruthlessness of their vision.

Aldous Huxley

Pretty much all the honest truth telling there is in the world is done by children.

Oscar Wilde

GENERATIONS
OF LOVE

When you look at your life, the greatest happinesses are family happinesses.

Dr. Joyce Brothers

Nobody can share a lifetime of experience and family legacies with a child the way a grandmother can.

Grandma Jan

Whatever their backgrounds or interests, grandmothers share common ground. They enjoy special family recipes or dishes, they share family jokes, common expressions or songs, and they participate in traditions and special events that bring the family together.

But most important of all, they're crazy about their grandchildren, and will go to the ends of the earth to play multiple roles as nurturers, caregivers, mentors, and wizards to them.

Grandma Jan

85

Over the river and through the wood.
  Now grandmother's cap I spy!

Hurray for the fun!
  Is the pudding done?
  Hurrah for the pumpkin pie!

Lydia Maria Child

Even a minor event in the life of a child is
an event of that child's world, and thus a
world event.

Gaston Bachelard

Listening children know stories are there.
When their elders sit and begin, children
are just waiting and hoping for one to come
out, like a mouse from a hole.

Eudora Welty

Some grandmas love to cook
Others prefer a good book

Some grandmas go to work each day
Others are retired and choose to play

Some grandmas are jolly and funny
Others are classy, loaded with money

Every grandma has a different face
All cherished in their special place

Deep in their grandchildren's hearts

Grandma Jan

My mother, now a great-grandmother, still
keeps all the children mesmerized with tales
of her escapades as a silent-screen extra.
With exciting stories of mobsters and the
stock market crash and vivid descriptions of
the clothing, entertainment, and headlines
of the time, she has recaptured a golden era
for three generations of family members.

Grandma Jan

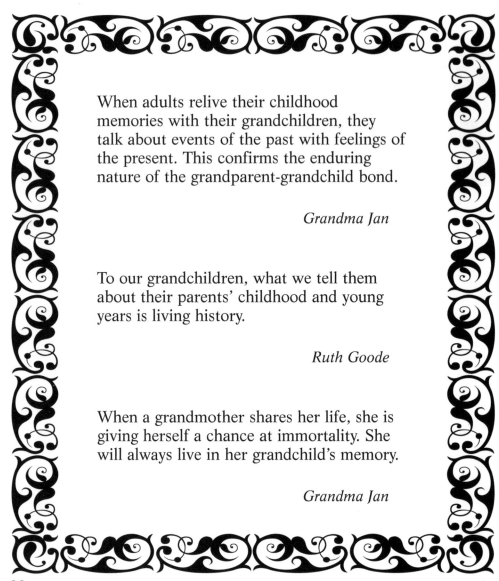

When adults relive their childhood memories with their grandchildren, they talk about events of the past with feelings of the present. This confirms the enduring nature of the grandparent-grandchild bond.

Grandma Jan

To our grandchildren, what we tell them about their parents' childhood and young years is living history.

Ruth Goode

When a grandmother shares her life, she is giving herself a chance at immortality. She will always live in her grandchild's memory.

Grandma Jan

My grandmother remembers with her heart
those tender little childhood moments that I
have long forgotten.

Joyce K. Allen Logan

From a Grateful Granddaughter

For as long as I can remember you were
always there
To teach me how to love others,
and how to love myself . . .
And to look for the good in everyone.
You were always there to listen,
to hold my hand, and to hug me.

Your joy for life and nurturing care
Have been a major influence in my life.

Thank you for being my grandmother.

Frieda McReynolds

Grandparents impart history and values by their very existence; it made the existence of their grandchildren possible.

Robert A. Aldrich, M.D.
and Glenn Austin, M.D.

Posterity is the patriotic name for grandchildren.

Art Linkletter

It is always self-defeating to pretend to the style of a generation younger than your own; it simply erases your own experience in history.

Renata Adler

The moment a baby is born, a grandmother is born too.

Grandma Jan

The birth of a grandchild is like the arrival of Spring, awakening from a deep Winter's sleep and budding forth with new life, bringing joy and optimism for the future.

Vera Allen-Smith

———————————

. . . I'm going to ask something of every one of you.

Let me start with my generation—the grandparents out there.

You are our living link to the past. Tell your grandchildren the story of the struggles waged, at home and abroad. Of sacrifices freely made for freedom's sake. And tell them your own story as well—because every American has a story to tell.

George Bush

Children are a great comfort in your old age—and they help you reach it faster too.

Lionel Kaufman

My Nana is awesome! She is the only one in my family who can boss my mom around and get away with it.

Jeffrey (age nine)

Any activity we enjoy with our grandchildren can become a family tradition: walks on the beach, playing charades, visiting a favorite ice-cream parlor, decorating Easter eggs, and even picking out a new pair of school shoes. These are events memories are made of, simple rituals which are passed from generation to generation.

Grandma Jan

As the years go by and my grandchildren grow older, I will no longer be in demand to baby-sit, read fairy tales, or ride the merry-go-round. How I dread that day! But if I'm lucky, there will be another time, another place, and other children. For someday I'll be a great-grandmother.

Grandma Jan

Nothing has the power to make you believe in miracles again like a new grandbaby.

Grandma Jan

A new grandbaby is about the size of a hug.

Grandma Jan

Loving Legacy

1. Begin showing small children photographs of themselves as babies and photos of other family members. Point out family resemblances and tell brief stories about the different pictures to help children develop a sense of belonging.

2. Tell stories from your childhood that have counterparts with situations in your grandchildren's lives.

3. Keep a journal, a kind of life-book. Even if children are not interested in hearing your stories and other family history now, they may be later.

4. Capture your grandchild's interest and imagination by bringing out memorabilia, such as yearbooks, records, souvenirs, clothing, and posters.

5. Consider making an audio or video tape of your life story or vignettes from your family's history.

6. Old folk songs and nursery rhymes are a wonderful way to communicate with youngsters. Sing them songs your mother taught you, the same ones they will teach their children.

Grandma Jan

You'll never forget when and where you first heard the news you had become a grandmother. All the joy wrapped up in that tiny bundle of love sparks a renewal in your relationship with your family that will be enhanced as the baby grows.

Grandma Jan

I suddenly realized that through no act of my own I had become biologically related to a new human being.

Margaret Mead

The joy of becoming a mother was a prelude to the elation of becoming a grandmother.

Vera Allen-Smith

Mrs. Margaret Thatcher informed the world with regal panache yesterday that her daughter-in-law had given birth to a son.

"We have become a grandmother," the Prime Minister said.

as quoted in the London Times, *March 4, 1989*

It was a thrill becoming a mother and a joy becoming a grandmother, but nothing can come close to the delight of becoming a great-grandmother.

Great-grandma Melé
Mother of Grandma Jan
Grandmother of Lance
Great-grandmother of Christopher,
Melanie, and Matthew

There is nothing more complimentary than wheeling your three-month-old grandson down the avenue and having a passerby ask if you're his mother.

Grandma Jan

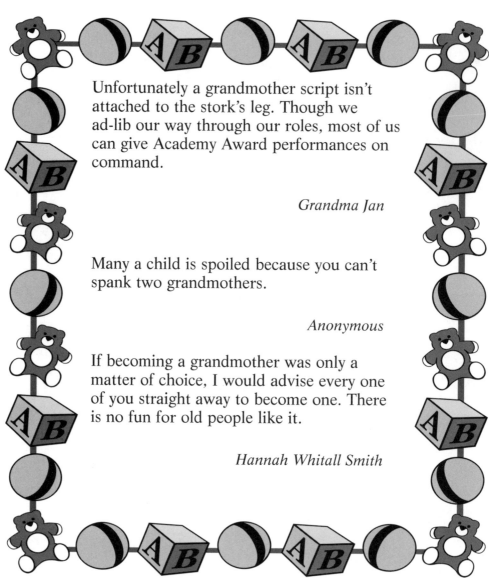

Unfortunately a grandmother script isn't attached to the stork's leg. Though we ad-lib our way through our roles, most of us can give Academy Award performances on command.

Grandma Jan

Many a child is spoiled because you can't spank two grandmothers.

Anonymous

If becoming a grandmother was only a matter of choice, I would advise every one of you straight away to become one. There is no fun for old people like it.

Hannah Whitall Smith

Once your children are grown up and have children of their own, the problems are theirs, and the less the older generation interferes the better.

Eleanor Roosevelt

No cowgirl was ever faster on the draw than a grandma pulling baby pictures out of her handbag.

Anonymous

You often meet grandparents who bore you about their grandchildren, but never vice versa.

Anonymous

You know a grandmother is a goner on her grandchild when she

❤ Nurses every sniffle as if were life-threatening

❤ Looks upon every crayon scrawl as creative genius

❤ Never misses a Little League game, recital, or spelling bee

❤ Insists she recognizes the potential of a "born leader"

❤ Makes up portfolios for talent agencies

❤ Frames all outstanding report cards

❤ Takes more family videos than the Kennedys

❤ Only goes to movies that are rated G

❤ Swears that *Goodnight Moon* is her favorite book

Grandma Jan

God gives us grandchildren so that we can undo some of the mistakes we made as parents.

Grandma Jan

———————

Grandmother: "Did I tell you about my grandchildren?"

Friend: "No, and I appreciate it very much."

Milton Berle

———————

Just about the time a woman thinks she can relax and take it easy, she becomes a grandmother.

Grandma Jan

A grandmother suspects she's entering her "golden years" when her husband orders a martini with a prune.

Anonymous

The largest segment of today's grandmothers is too young to take up croquet and too old to rush the net.

Grandma Jan

The three stages of grandmotherhood—youthful, mature, and "you're looking wonderful!"

Grandma Jan

To a grandmother of a ten-year-old linebacker, any football game he plays in becomes a nervous breakdown divided into quarters.

Grandma Jan

My favorite sweatshirt was a gift from my daughter-in-law Marie. In big, bold letters it announces that I am a

PROUD MEMBER OF THE GRANDMA CLUB

Grandma Jan

Even if you have resisted the idea of becoming a grandmother, you'll soon find it is one of life's greatest joys. Gazing into that sweet innocent face, grasping those tiny, soft hands, rocking a tiny bundle of joy who is a loving extension of you; what a midlife ecstasy!

Grandma Jan

GRANDMA JAN SAYS

It's a wise grandmother who understands her strengths and weaknesses and helps her grandchildren to understand their own.

Grandma Jan

Grandchildren come into our lives, bask in our love, and return it to us in their special ways. Yet we cannot live through them. Like our children they are not ours to own; they belong to the world. We must give our grandchildren wings and teach them to fly.

Grandma Jan

The best way a grandmother can get her grandchildren to listen to her is to listen to them.

Grandma Jan

A grandma can expand her grandchild's view of the universe.

Grandma Jan

The most valued grandmother asks her children and grandchildren "What can I do for you?" and then does it.

Grandma Jan

A loving grandmother doesn't compare her grandchildren to others. She values each of them for their own special gifts.

Grandma Jan

The greatest gift you can give your grandchild is yourself.

Grandma Jan

Grandmothering holds the greatest rewards for those who put their best efforts into it.

Grandma Jan

Already people over sixty-five outnumber teenagers. As their numbers increase, grandmothers will be powerful spokeswomen in the twenty-first century. Our children and grandchildren look to us for leadership. Being the best we can provides them with positive role models.

Grandma Jan

Grandparenting is an education.
Grandparents and grandchildren learn from
one another.

Grandma Jan

One grandmother is worth a hundred
educators.

Grandma Jan

A grandma doesn't need a Ph.D. in Child
Development to be a great teacher. Her
grandchildren learn by emulating the person
they admire the most.

Grandma Jan

arents are those who learn from their parents.

Grandma Jan

Most grandmothers are proud of the way their children are rearing their grandchildren in today's difficult society. Unfortunately their words of approval are rarely voiced. A little praise goes a long way toward a closer bond and a deeper trust between grandparents and parents.

Grandma Jan

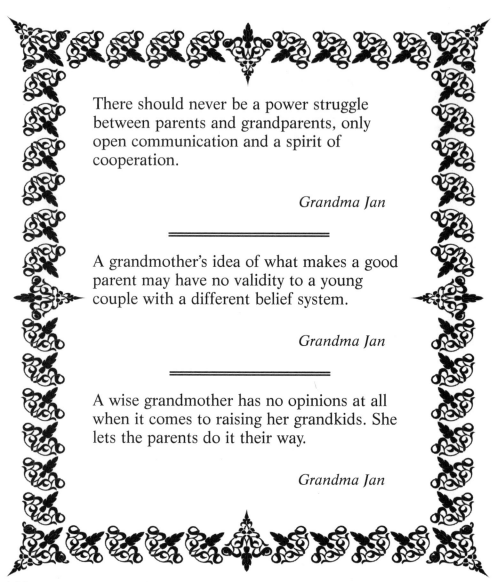

There should never be a power struggle
between parents and grandparents, only
open communication and a spirit of
cooperation.

Grandma Jan

A grandmother's idea of what makes a good
parent may have no validity to a young
couple with a different belief system.

Grandma Jan

A wise grandmother has no opinions at all
when it comes to raising her grandkids. She
lets the parents do it their way.

Grandma Jan

You'll hit the top of the parent popularity
parade if you give your adult children

1. Respect

2. Acceptance

3. Understanding

4. Support

5. Love

6. Advice (only when asked)

7. Encouragement

8. Appreciation

9. Help

10. Praise

Grandma Jan

You'll plummet to the bottom of the popularity list if you show them

1. Irreverence

2. Superiority

3. Contention

4. Opposition

5. Scorn

6. Interference

7. Judgment

8. Belittlement

9. Indifference

10. Criticism

Grandma Jan

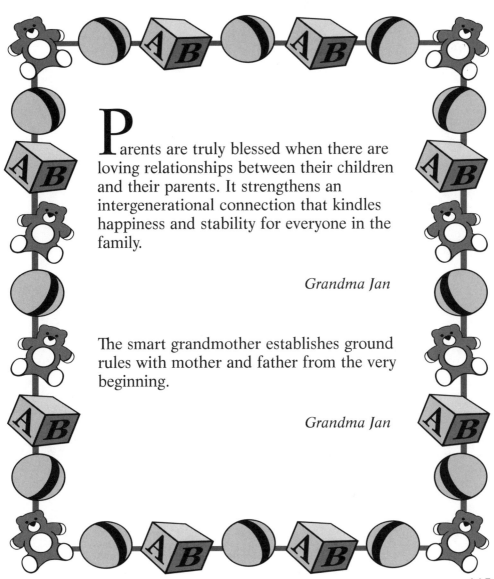

Parents are truly blessed when there are loving relationships between their children and their parents. It strengthens an intergenerational connection that kindles happiness and stability for everyone in the family.

Grandma Jan

The smart grandmother establishes ground rules with mother and father from the very beginning.

Grandma Jan

115

The best way for a grandmother to stay young is to live honestly, work industriously, exercise regularly, eat sensibly, sleep sufficiently, and avoid telling her age.

Grandma Jan

You don't need to be a super grandma for your grandkids to cherish you. One treasured memory can last a lifetime.

Grandma Jan

Long-distance grandparenting is possible!
The miles can be bridged with phone calls,
photos, letters, tapes, videos, and a monthly
supply of homemade goodies.

Grandma Jan

Lap time with your grandchild is quality
time.

Grandma Jan

Janet Lanese is a perfect example of a grandmother of the nineties. She combines multiple careers as a real estate broker, a writer for her community newspaper, a co-hostess for a local television program, and a contributing editor for over thirty parenting and religious magazines. Janet Lanese lives in Castro Valley, California, and, even with her busy schedule, she finds time to enjoy her three grandchildren.